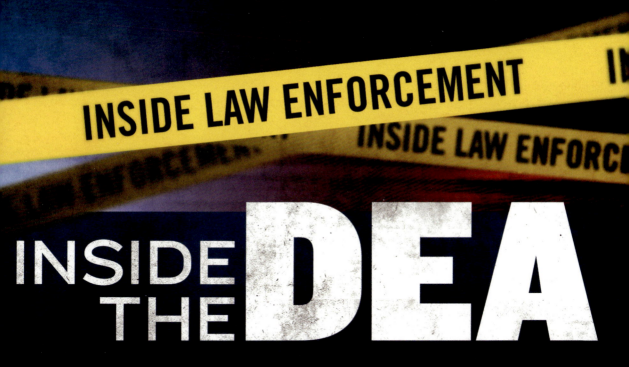

INSIDE LAW ENFORCEMENT

INSIDE THE DEA

Bridey Heing

Enslow Publishing
101 W. 23rd Street
Suite 240
New York, NY 10011
USA

enslow.com

Published in 2020 by Enslow Publishing, LLC.
101 W. 23rd Street, Suite 240, New York, NY 10011

Copyright © 2020 by Enslow Publishing, LLC.

All rights reserved.

No part of this book may be reproduced by any means without the written permission of the publisher.

Library of Congress Cataloging-in-Publication Data

Names: Heing, Bridey, author.
Title: Inside the DEA / Bridey Heing.
Description: New York : Enslow Publishing, 2020. | Series: Inside law enforcement | Includes bibliographical references and index. | Audience: Grades 5-8.
Identifiers: LCCN 2018058101| ISBN 9781978507340 (library bound) | ISBN 9781978508538 (pbk.)
Subjects: LCSH: United States. Drug Enforcement Administration—Juvenile literature. | Drug control—United States—Juvenile literature. | Drug traffic—United States—Juvenile literature.
Classification: LCC HV5825 .H36 2020 | DDC 363.28/40973—dc23
LC record available at https://lccn.loc.gov/2018058101

Printed in the United States of America

To Our Readers: We have done our best to make sure all website addresses in this book were active and appropriate when we went to press. However, the author and the publisher have no control over and assume no liability for the material available on those websites or on any websites they may link to. Any comments or suggestions can be sent by email to customerservice@enslow.com.

Photo Credits: Cover, pp. 1, 18 Portland Press Herald/Getty Images; p. 5 AB Forces News Collection/Alamy Stock Photo; pp. 8, 22, 32 © AP Images; p. 11 Focus on Sport/Getty Images; p. 13 Bettmann/Getty Images; pp. 14, 40 John Moore/Getty Images; p. 21 Paul J. Richards/AFP/Getty Images; p. 25 Cris Bouroncle/AFP/Getty Images; p. 26 Reza/Getty Images; p. 28 Wiktor Dabkowski/picturealliance/dpa/AP Images; p. 34 Pedro Pardo/AFP/Getty Images; p. 36 Fredy Amariles/AFP/Getty Images; p. 39 Brendan Smialowski/AFP/Getty Images.

CONTENTS

Introduction 4

Chapter 1 A History of the DEA............................ 7

Chapter 2 The Duties of the DEA 17

Chapter 3 The DEA Overseas............................ 24

Chapter 4 Controversies of the DEA 31

Chapter 5 The Future of the DEA 38

Chapter Notes.. 43

Glossary 44

Further Reading.. 46

Index 47

INTRODUCTION

For law enforcement, controlling the distribution and use of illegal drugs is important for reasons that go far beyond the criminality of doing some illicit substances. Illegal drug use can lead to other forms of criminal activity: robbery can be used as a means to obtain money to buy drugs, murder is common among those who deal drugs on a large scale, and the impaired judgement that comes with drug use can lead to unintentional but no less critical crimes being committed. Due to this significant overlap, there are a few agencies that work on drug control. But there is only one that focuses solely on enforcing the laws surrounding drug sales and use: the Drug Enforcement Administration.

The Drug Enforcement Administration was created by President Richard Nixon in 1973 as a way to centralize drug control efforts. The creation of the DEA came at a time when drug use was on the rise and the nature of drugs was changing, becoming more synthetic and dangerous. The DEA was set up in part as a response to the 1970 passage of the Controlled Substances Act, which established our current system of drug classification and punishment for importing or exporting substances that are scheduled according to that classification system. The DEA, along with the Food and Drug Administration (FDA), is responsible for scheduling substances according to the CSA.

Since its founding, the DEA has become a powerful agency that plays a part not just in enforcing US drug laws, but in monitoring and targeting

The Drug Enforcement Administration, or DEA, is responsible for enforcing drug laws and stopping the spread of illegal drugs within the United States. That includes not only dealing with US dealers but anyone who sends drugs to the United States from other countries.

those who funnel drugs to the US from other countries. DEA leadership, including the administrator of drug enforcement, reports to the attorney general. They provide information on investigations and operations. These operations can include raids, arrests, or other activities intended to stop the spread of illegal drugs.

The DEA is also responsible for overseas operations. Along with twenty-one offices in the United States, there are DEA offices in about seventy different countries. Through these offices, the DEA targets cartels and leadership who oversee the transport and sale of high volumes of drugs to the United States. That can include organized crime leaders and governments, which are targeted through sting operations and intelligence-gathering efforts, such as espionage.

But the DEA has also been involved in significant controversies. Particularly in regards to its operations overseas, the DEA has been accused of overstepping in its efforts to find and target drug offenders and dealers. Its methods have also called into question its effectiveness—accusations against the agency range from advocating for extreme zero-tolerance policies to wrongful imprisonment to corruption.

Over the course of four decades, the DEA has become one of the most influential forces in drug law enforcement, working with agencies as diverse as the Federal Bureau of Investigation (FBI) and the Department of Homeland Security (DHS) to target criminals both domestically and internationally. This book will look at how the DEA developed, the role it plays in law enforcement, and what the future might hold for this storied agency.

CHAPTER 1

A HISTORY OF THE DEA

The Drug Enforcement Administration was established to deal with a problem that had long plagued the United States—narcotics, particularly the use and sale of narcotics. The DEA was not the first agency to be responsible for implementing US drug law. From the earliest days of drug policy in the United States, there has been an international component to both the work of creating laws and enforcing those laws. As a result, the work of the DEA has changed in practice over the decades, but not in nature.

Before the DEA

Although the DEA was established in 1973, the United States began introducing drug laws as early as 1906. That year, the Pure Food and Drug Act became law, which mandated that products made with cocaine and heroin were to be clearly labeled. At the turn of the 20th century,

Most people think of raids like this one when they think of the DEA, but in addition to stopping the spread of illegal drugs, it works to prevent legal drugs from being sold on the black market in the US.

heroin and cocaine were both common ingredients in medicine and patent medicine, made and sold by people with little to no medical training and bought without a prescription. The easy access to cocaine and heroin, both of which are highly addictive, was a major public health concern, and the labeling of these products was meant to help consumers make informed decisions.

In 1914, the Harrison Narcotics Tax Act went a step further by regulating and imposing a tax on products made with opium and cocaine, or coca. Opium, which had been used widely in medicine, was restricted to only the treatment of non-addiction-related disorders. What's more, taxes were levied against those who sold or made drugs made of coca and required those who did so to register with the government. Today, the law is seen as the beginning of the United States' efforts to bar the use of narcotics.

It also created the link between the Bureau of Internal Revenue, the forerunner to the Internal Revenue Service (IRS), and drug enforcement. It was the Bureau of Internal Revenue that carried out the enforcement and investigation of Prohibition, which required agents to identify and shut down large- and small-scale alcohol sales operations. Bureaus within the Department of the Treasury, including the Bureau of Prohibition and the Bureau of Narcotics, oversaw drug regulation and enforcement (along with the short-lived Bureau of Drug Abuse Control in the FDA) until 1968, when the Bureau of Narcotics and Dangerous Drugs was established within the Department of Justice. With a limited budget and a small staff, however, the BNDD was replaced about five years after it was established with the DEA, a centralized agency that could focus on a comprehensive drug control agenda.

Controlled Substances Act

The passage of the Controlled Substances Act in 1971 set the stage for the DEA. Although other legislation designed to reduce the use of drugs like marijuana had already been passed, the CSA was the first legislation to broadly ban the use of drugs. The CSA established our modern drug scheduling system, by which drugs are categorized based on addictiveness and potential for abuse, among other criteria. Drugs belonging to Schedule 1, for example, are the most heavily regulated. These drugs are believed to have no medical use, and therefore all use is banned by federal law. Along with use, the CSA bars the study of these drugs, which include hallucinogens and heroin. The lowest categorization is Schedule V, which includes cough syrups and some over-the-counter medications that include opiates.

Two years after the passage of the CSA, President Richard Nixon began advocating for the establishment of a centralized agency to oversee drug control. The DEA was approved by Congress in 1973. The DEA was designed to help overcome a few obstacles that had made enforcing regulations on drug use and sale difficult, including rivalry between agencies with some oversight of drug policy and the difficulty in coordinating multiple task forces and operations across the country. It would also make it easier for the US to coordinate and work with international allies by providing a focal point for contact, and create a more effective system of drug regulation by centralizing power with one administrator. The agency would also work as an intelligence agency, focusing on drug-related activities both in the United States and overseas.

Once established, the DEA moved fast to break ground on its new mandate. The agency set up training programs, began coordinating with international allies, collected intelligence on leading drug-related figures (including Timothy Leary, a counterculture figure who advocated for the use of psychotropic drugs like LSD), and integrating new technology to ensure the DEA was on the cutting edge.

Unlike other agencies, which sometimes have to fight for their place in the law enforcement landscape, the DEA was staffed and funded fully from the beginning, which made it a force to be reckoned with as soon as it was established. Its activities only grew as the 1970s gave way to the 1980s, as presidents focused more and more on the epidemics of drug use during those two decades. The agency began working on prevention, particularly working to educate children on the dangers of drug use, a

Among the DEA's antidrug efforts were campaigns to help kids understand the dangers of drugs, like the 1980s' "Just Say No" campaign headed by First Lady Nancy Reagan.

project that was bolstered by First Lady Nancy Reagan's "Just Say No" campaign in the early 1980s.

Red Ribbon Campaign

By the mid-1980s, the DEA was the domestic leader in drug control enforcement. But that won it enemies—and in some cases, powerful enemies. The agency was especially active in South America, where much of the United States' cocaine originated. In the 1980s, the high supply of cocaine led to the development of crack, which is more addictive and dangerous than cocaine. The use of crack reached epidemic levels by the mid-1980s, and as such the DEA's efforts to stem the flow of cocaine into the United States increased.

In 1985, however, the murder of Special Agent Enrique Camarena threw a light on the dangers of the DEA's work. He was killed by drug traffickers, and his death sparked the Red Ribbon Campaign. The campaign was designed to encourage people to live drug-free lives, particularly high school students. The intention was to reduce the demand for drugs like cocaine, using prevention as a means to do so.

THE WAR ON DRUGS

Drug policy in the United States began taking shape in the early 20th century, with President Richard Nixon taking decisive action to create an overarching strategy to combat drug use and sale. Nixon also popularized the term "war on drugs," a phrase he used to describe the attention his administration planned to give combating narcotics. But it wasn't until 1982, with President Ronald Reagan, that the "war on drugs" truly came to the forefront. Under the Reagan administration, money and resources were poured into the DEA and other agencies to more specifically go after drug-related targets, including the incarceration of nonviolent and first-time offenders. The incarcerations, and the racial disparity in those arrested, increased under the Clinton administration, which put in place mandatory minimum sentencing for most drug-related crimes. Under President Barack Obama, it was announced the controversial term "war on drugs" would no longer be used, although policies on drug control remained much the same.

Officers who work for the DEA often track drugs that have entered the country through illegal entry points, such as along the US-Mexico border.

The late 1980s saw a flurry of drug control legislation, including the Anti-Drug Abuse Act of 1986. This bill authorized $6 billion over the course of three years to increase enforcement of existing laws while increasing prevention and education initiatives. In 1988, another Anti-Drug Abuse Act was passed, introducing higher criminal penalties for drug-related offenses.

One of the biggest drug cartels was run by Manuel Noriega, a former military and political leader in Panama who trafficked drugs through his country to the United States.

Targeting Trafficking

While domestic efforts were focused on controlling the sale of drugs and preventing the spread of their use, the DEA was also responsible for stopping the flow of drugs altogether by stopping traffickers. This international component was an important part of drug regulation from the early 1900s, as bootlegging operations during Prohibition were often based on the import of illegal alcohol and opium from Asia and other parts of the world. Controlling that stream of narcotics thus became one of the core focuses of the DEA when it was established in the early 1970s.

Gathering intelligence and sting operations were two ways in which the DEA immediately began targeting international trafficking. But about a decade after it was established, the agency became more aggressive in how it handled international cases. The DEA carried out several high-profile missions during the late 1980s, including securing the extradition of drug kingpin Carlos Lehder from Colombia and arresting Manuel Noriega, a Panamanian military leader who assisted in shipping cocaine between the United States and Colombia.

In 1987, the DEA began Operation Snowcap, which remains one of the largest efforts the agency carried out. Coordinating with the State Department's Bureau of International Narcotics Matters, the mission focused on the cocaine industry by targeting twelve countries, including Guatemala, Panama, Colombia, Ecuador, Mexico, and Peru. The mission continued until 1994 and involved breaking up transit lines for major drug cartels. Tons of cocaine were seized, hundreds of facilities used for processing and storage were destroyed, and thousands of traffickers were arrested.

In 1992, DEA chief Robert Bonner introduced the Kingpin Strategy, a new direction for the DEA's work overseas. The strategy shifted focus toward the highest-priority targets in drug cartels—the so-called

Kingpins. By targeting leadership, the DEA hoped cartels like the Colombian Cali and Medellin cartels would crumble without these central figures. But the Kingpin Strategy didn't really have an impact. While it broke up large cartels, it didn't stem the flow of drugs into the country in a meaningful way, particularly as smaller operations or those with links to paramilitaries in South America began to fill in where the once-powerful cartels had fallen.

Today, the DEA's efforts are still largely focused on the southern border, although operations in the 2000s also targeted opium in Afghanistan and efforts to smuggle marijuana and other drugs between the US and Canada. Its initiatives have also had to take into account concerns like the opioid epidemic in the United States, changing state legislation around marijuana, and other changes in our understanding of drug use.

CHAPTER 2

THE DUTIES OF THE DEA

The DEA has a broad mandate to oversee and enforce drug-related regulations, as well as find new ways to prevent the use of illicit substances in the United States. Doing so means working in numerous fields and wearing many different hats. But all of the duties that fall under the DEA's umbrella fit together when one looks at them through the lens of drug control, a field that demands innovative and ever-evolving practices.

Education

Education plays a large role in the DEA's work. Although targeting those who are already smuggling, selling, and using drugs is a significant task of the DEA, part of reducing drug use is ensuring the demand goes down across the country. This means the DEA must educate the public on the dangers of drug use, the consequences one faces, and ways to avoid falling into addiction.

To help stop the spread of illegal drugs, the DEA runs programs like DARE (Drug Abuse Resistance Education) with local law enforcement agencies to educate kids and young adults.

Much of its community outreach involves communicating with young people, especially through schools. Community outreach includes drug fact sheets and education for adults, like teachers and parents, who could be able to recognize patterns that suggest drug use in young people. By partnering with other government agencies, schools, and community groups, the DEA tries to reach as many young people—or others in need of information—as possible.

Community outreach can also include supporting rehabilitation programs. The agency partners with and registers addiction treatment programs, funds adult education programs for both recovering addicts and their families, and supports programs that help recovering addicts avoid relapse.

Investigation

One of the most important parts of the DEA's work is investigation. Arresting those who are selling drugs on a low level makes a difference; however, the DEA must focus on breaking up the systems by which drugs are produced and transferred, which means taking out entire operations. The DEA's information is also important for the subsequent court cases that bring offenders to justice. Doing so requires a great deal of accurate, reliable information, which isn't always easy to get.

In some cases, the DEA is able to gain informants, or people who would otherwise be working a cartel or other operation but agree to provide information to the DEA and other law enforcement agencies in exchange for a reduced sentence or immunity. In other cases, the DEA sends an agent in undercover to work with a cartel or operation, to gain a full insider's perspective. Both of these actions are dangerous—drug smugglers or cartels can be violent and might kill or otherwise harm someone they find out is betraying them. So the DEA must be extra cautious with communication, often requiring undercover agents to behave as if they are fully part of the operation they are gathering intelligence on.

There are other means by which the DEA can gain intelligence, though. It might listen in on conversations or intercept communications, interrogate those it has arrested to get a sense of who else might be targeted, or carry out what is called forensic financial analysis. That is when the DEA or other law enforcement agencies track specific dollar bills to get a sense of how they are being spent, where, and between whom. By doing so, agents can map out supply chains and gain an understanding of how drugs are being sold from person to person, as well as keep track of trends in how groups of dealers and traffickers, such as cartels, operate.

Coordination

The DEA is the only agency with the sole mandate to oversee drug-related regulation, but it isn't the only agency that does so. The FBI also shares some of the burden, while state and local law enforcement have their own task forces for dealing with drug abuse and dealing. There are also international partners with which the DEA works, particularly on gathering intelligence and enforcing laws that would diminish the supply of drugs to the United States.

WORKING FOR THE DEA

Like many high-profile law enforcement agencies, the DEA is seen as far more simple than it is, particularly in regards to career opportunities. While the DEA does hire professionals to carry out raids and other operations that look like traditional law enforcement, there is far more that goes into a career in the DEA than carrying a gun. In fact, the DEA hires all kinds of experts—and provides training programs so that talented candidates can learn all the ins and outs of working for this agency. Career paths include becoming a special agent, an investigator, or an intelligence specialist, among others. Candidates need a bachelor's degree and need to pass a written assessment before being interviewed, then are required to take particular training programs. From there, a career can take many forms, all while serving the DEA's larger mission of helping to eradicate the illegal drug market.

Drug-sniffing dogs are one of the many tools the DEA has at its disposal to help officers track down drugs and drug dealers across the country.

Coordinating these efforts isn't easy. In most cases, states within the United States and foreign countries don't have set methods to share information about possible drug dealers, organized crime, or other possible people of interest. Even information about arrests isn't always shared from county to county, let alone between the United States and an allied nation. But that is the kind of information that can create real breakthroughs in investigations. Fostering cooperation among so many different groups requires careful planning, respect for jurisdictions, and the work of establishing mutual trust.

While not all of the DEA's work makes headlines, major drug busts, like this one in Miami in 1999, make the news because of the sheer volume of drugs found. In this case, it was $20 million worth of cocaine.

THE DUTIES OF THE DEA

In addition to coordinating these efforts, the DEA is responsible for working with international organizations like Interpol and the United Nations. These organizations, which often have their own teams and task forces focused on drug-related concerns, can help assist in coordinating with countries the United States might not normally have diplomatic relations with, or sharing other insider knowledge that can help make coordination simpler.

Enforcement

The DEA is responsible for the task of enforcing drug laws, particularly the Controlled Substances Act. Agents do this in several ways. They carry out arrests and stings, as well as assess forfeiture operations. They also organize task forces, through which they partner with local law enforcement across the country to carry out localized operations with the help of DEA resources.

Enforcement is largely carried out by the DEA Special Operations Division and might see the DEA partner with Homeland Security, the FDA, or Immigration and Customs Enforcement. It might also partner with the military on international operations, such as in Afghanistan. DEA agents who carry out enforcement operations are usually heavily armed and backed up by a significant number of fellow agents. In some operations even aircraft assist, particularly on missions targeting large-scale targets.

The DEA has one mission: eradicate illegal drug use in the United States. Doing so takes more than just police activity. It takes education, coordination, and careful planning of missions that will not only bring criminals to justice, but also provide important intelligence to help agents understand the ecosystem in which drug operations flourish.

CHAPTER 3

THE DEA OVERSEAS

The DEA's work crosses borders in more ways than one. Just as the agency has to coordinate and partner with agencies and law enforcement across state lines, it needs to work with countries around the world to ensure their work is effective and correctly targeting those most responsible for drug trafficking. That's because drug trafficking is truly global in scope. Drugs often originate in one country, pass through others, and end up being sold in nations around the world—including the United States.

South America, Central America, and Mexico

South America has been a focus of the DEA for multiple decades, particularly as narco-gangs began flourishing there in the 1970s, 1980s, and early 1990s. Cocaine originates in several countries to the south and is

In addition to its work in the United States, the DEA works with foreign law enforcement agencies to help capture drug traffickers who sell to US dealers.

INSIDE THE DEA

In the Middle East, the DEA works with local law enforcement to try to slow down the opium trade. Opium is made from poppies, which grow abundantly in places like Afghanistan.

brought north via a few routes, including by air and by land through the Caribbean or Mexico.

The DEA has offices across the region based on geographic location and particular focus. The Andean region is comprised of Colombia, Ecuador, and Venezuela, with a focus on heroin and cocaine production and distribution. The Southern Cone is made up of the rest of South America, with a focus on distribution rather than production. For the North and Central American offices, there is a more significant cluster of operations in Central America and Mexico than farther north into the United States and Canada, focusing on production and distribution of cocaine, methamphetamine, heroin, and marijuana.

The Middle East

The Middle East has emerged since 2000 as a hotbed of drug-related activity. Like South and Central America, cartels have developed in places with weak governance, including Afghanistan. But unlike South and Central America, the Middle East is covered entirely by what the DEA calls "a few" offices, with Russia and other countries beyond what we would traditionally consider the Middle East included in the region.

The Middle East is active in the trade of opium, the drug that is used to produce heroin. In fact, the region is the primary supplier of opium. This was something that entered the public consciousness after the beginning of the US war in Afghanistan, which threw a spotlight not just on the production of opium but also on the closely interrelated nature of the drug trade, terrorism, and even governance. The drug trade is especially complicated in the region due to ongoing conflict, corruption, and the involvement of terrorist organizations, which use the drug trade as a source of income.

INSIDE THE DEA

The DEA also works in Europe, where "party drugs" like ecstasy are popular. By working with local drug enforcement groups, it can stop drug dealers before the drugs get to the United States.

    The Middle East is also a common transit space, with more heroin and opium coming from East and South Asia into Europe, Africa, and North America. These drugs pose unique challenges for the DEA and other agencies, due in part to their use in conflict spaces. Child soldiers in Africa and Asia, as well as the Middle East, are sometimes given opium

THE DEA OVERSEAS

to make them more docile and easier to control, making breaking up the drug-trafficking networks all the more important.

Europe

Although Europe is not a large producer of drugs, the continent is an important focus of drug transit and a destination for cocaine, opium, and other drugs from beyond its borders. Drugs like ecstasy are also common, and can be transported to the United States and other destinations from Europe. The DEA has offices across the region, and partners with governments and nongovernmental organizations (NGOs) to target trafficking operations.

THE MEDELLIN CARTEL

Since the 1980s, the DEA has focused significantly on cartels working in South America, especially those trafficking in cocaine. One of those cartels was the Medellin cartel, a famed trafficking organization that rose to prominence in the 1980s. Run by Pablo Escobar and based in Colombia, the Medellin cartel was responsible for the deaths of untold numbers of people, political unrest, and strengthening the narcotics trade in a way that did lasting damage to Colombian security. He is believed to have played a part in the bombing of an airplane and a truck bombing of the Administrative Department of Security in Bogota in 1989, and the 1985 siege of the Palace of Justice. But Escobar is also remembered as a hero of sorts. He grew up poor, devoted a great deal of money to the impoverished area of Medellin where he once lived, and was elected to Colombia's Chamber of Representatives. The DEA played a role in Search Bloc, the interagency organization that eventually killed Escobar in a shootout in 1993. At its height, the Medellin cartel brought in around $70 million per day, but after the death of Escobar, other cartels began to rise to power.

Europe, being a transit point and destination, offers the DEA the chance to understand how organized crime units work in the context of this part of the world. The European Union struggles to contain organized crime, which is sustained in part by the profits of the drug trade. Bringing in cocaine and other drugs from around the world, mobs and gangs in the region are able to generate significant income, connecting organized crime in Europe to cartels and other syndicates around the world. Breaking up these large, well-connected and, in many cases, extremely wealthy organizations offers the chance to target smaller operations around the world, and to gain a sense of how these networks come together and can be broken up in the future.

CHAPTER 4

CONTROVERSIES OF THE DEA

The DEA, like other law enforcement agencies, has had a sometimes troubled history with issues of transparency and accountability. The agency has been accused of violating the human rights of those it targets, and it has been kicked out of countries where it was once active due to allegations of misconduct. While the work of the DEA is important, it is just as important that the controversies surrounding the organization be fully understood to make way for reforms to ensure that it works in an ethical way.

Domestic Misconduct

The DEA is responsible for carrying out raids and other operations to target and bring to justice drug dealers around the country. But not all of its practices are seen as ethical. In fact, the agency has a history of targeting the wrong people or overlooking innocent bystanders. In 2012,

While the DEA does its best to stop the illegal drug trade, it is not without its controversies, such as mistreatment of detainees and racist policies.

a twenty-four year old was arrested during a raid and held for five days without food or water, despite not being charged. Following an attempted suicide, the young man was released and the DEA was eventually made to pay $4.1 million to him as a result of a lawsuit. The DEA also has been responsible for killing innocent people believed to be part of drug-related operations and for raiding the wrong homes.[1]

There are concerns about the racial disparity of DEA raids and activities. Non-white targets are far more common than white targets, and as a result more people of color go to prison for drug-related offenses than white people do. This is despite studies that have found drug use and dealing are just as common across races, or in some cases more likely to be done by white people. The DEA's stringent guidelines on drug-related offenses has long been singled out as creating a system in which those

THE DEA AND MARIJUANA

Marijuana was one of the first drugs to be regulated in the United States and has been a Schedule I drug since the DEA began categorizing narcotics. But today, our understanding of marijuana is changing rapidly, with some states even legalizing the use and sale of marijuana or marijuana-derived products. This poses an interesting and sometimes confusing conflict: while marijuana becomes legal around the country and has been legal in many places for years as a medical treatment, the drug remains illegal under federal law. Marijuana being a Schedule I drug provides heavy punishments for those caught selling or using it under federal jurisdiction, a policy that has drawn criticism as it places people behind bars even as the drug is legalized. But the DEA is also beginning to change its stance on marijuana. Although it remains illegal and the agency focuses on eradication of the drug in the United States, some medical treatments derived from cannabis are being scheduled lower, including as Schedule V substances.

While marijuana is medically or recreationally legal in some places, it is still not federally legal in the United States, which means the DEA is still responsible for stopping illegal sales of the drug.

who are arrested are given few if any leniency—and in too many cases that seems to create an unfair burden on communities of color.[2]

International Actions

The DEA's relationships in South America, Central America, and Mexico have been fraught at times. Narcotics particularly caused political unrest in South America, and more recently in Central America, with governments destabilized by both the narco-trade and by American influence over their political structure. Today, the DEA partners closely with government organizations and NGOs. It is important to remember that demand for drugs in the United States is part of what fuels the drug trade in this and other parts of the world, and that relations between the US and South America have long been complicated by power imbalances.

Bolivia is a country where the DEA has long had fraught relations with leadership, including President Evo Morales, who kicked the DEA out of his country in 2008. Since then, the DEA has worked to suggest that Morales and his inner circle are involved in the cocaine trade, allegations the DEA's critics say are just fabricated to get back at Morales for rejecting its effort to partner with him.[3] In Colombia, in 2017, the DEA was rocked by allegations of misconduct that ranged from working with drug cartels to engaging in activities barred by the DEA.[4] Anecdotal concerns like these are part of a much larger pattern that includes mission creep and allegations of interference in local governance. While the DEA's work is important and global by nature, so, too, is the sovereignty of the countries where it operates and the integrity of the agency as a whole, which is threatened by misconduct and other unethical practices.

Lack of Accountability

All the concerns related to the DEA boil down to one central worry: that holding an agency like the DEA, which has a broad mandate and an internal culture that prioritizes the mission at hand, accountable can be nearly impossible. Allegations of a lack of oversight, particularly in relation to its work in South America, have long plagued the agency, while there are worries that individual agents that are accused of misconduct are not suitably investigated.[5]

INSIDE THE DEA

Colombia is well known for producing a large amount of the illegal drugs that make it to the United States. That is why the agency works closely with South American and Central American law enforcement.

CONTROVERSIES OF THE DEA

This isn't a unique challenge. In fact, it's fairly common for law enforcement agencies to weather and respond to concerns about accountability. This is in part due to the secretive nature of much of their work and to the high stakes involved in their missions. But it is important that all law enforcement agencies work within the constraints of the law and in a way that affirms their role as serving the public, rather than doing damage to communities or, in the case of the DEA, foreign countries. The DEA's slow response—or even refusal to respond—to these concerns is one area in which the agency must reform if it is to remain an effective tool working for the betterment of public health through eradicating drug use.

CHAPTER 5

THE FUTURE OF THE DEA

Upon its founding in 1973, the Drug Enforcement Administration was tasked with regulating drug scheduling and stemming the spread of drug use in the United States. Since then, the agency has become not just a national leader in fighting drug abuse, but also an important international partner for organizations and governments around the world. It has been on the cutting edge of technological innovation in law enforcement, served as an important gatherer and analyst of intelligence, and forged relationships that have helped bring criminals around the world to justice.

Despite the founded concerns of its critics, the DEA remains an integral part of US law enforcement at home and abroad. Working with the FBI, CIA, military, and other agencies related to justice, the DEA has proven time and again that its coordination and planning are important facets of bringing criminals to justice. What's more, its work

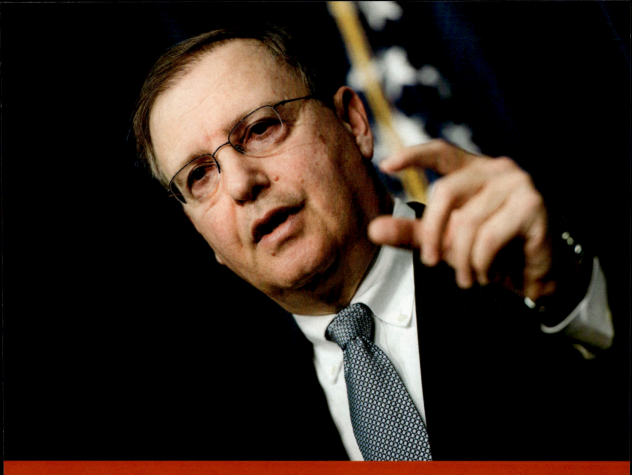

In 2017, then-DEA administrator Chuck Rosenberg discussed the dangers of the opioid epidemic, a drug problem that, in 2019, caused more than 130 overdose deaths per day.

focuses not just on small operations, but on large ones that disrupt governments, harm untold thousands of people each year, and leave countries in danger of collapse. Meanwhile, at home, it helps educate the public to decrease the demand for narcotics—an important and not-to-be-overlooked facet of its work.

In 2018, the DEA announced a new initiative called the 360 Strategy. Designed to tackle the growing issue of opioid abuse in the United States, the 360 Strategy is intended to build on the DEA's comprehensive work in education, investigation, and law enforcement with a focus on

In 2018, activists headed to Washington, DC, to ask the government to devote more money and resources to ending the opioid epidemic.

THE DEA AND SURVEILLANCE

One of the largest questions hanging over national law enforcement is the question of ethical surveillance. Along with numerous other law enforcement and intelligence agencies in the United States, the DEA has been part of leaked revelations that indicate the use of mass surveillance of US citizens and targets abroad. These practices, though not illegal in all cases, are of questionable morality and ethics—but many sign away privacy rights in relation to data and other online tools when signing up for social media. The DEA has been accused of using surveillance, including information gained from the NSA, to identify targets and make arrests. But some worry this is an overstep and that the DEA must be held accountable for infringing on privacy. As of now, the practice continues. However, it is unclear how much of an impact mass surveillance has on the DEA's operations—or whether the agency will give up using these increasingly available pools of data.

heroin and opioids. Although opium and heroin were among the very first drugs the US tried to regulate, today's battle is much different than it was in the early 1900s. Prescription opioids of today are a huge concern due to their highly addictive nature, ease of access, and threat of overdose. By working with hospitals, as well as law enforcement partners and educational partners, the DEA hopes to stem the growing use of opioids around the country. As Louisville-based Special Agent in Charge D. Christopher Evans explained, "DEA is working closely with many agencies and organizations that deal separately with these problems and merging them into a unified, comprehensive and sustained initiative to target drug traffickers and restore local communities to a safe and healthy state."[1]

INSIDE THE DEA

The DEA of the future, like the DEA of the past, will likely continue finding ways to expand on its central work. What is fascinating about working to eradicate drug trafficking and use is how little it truly changes over time. From the earliest days of drug regulation, similar challenges have presented themselves in regard to doing so. From the international nature of drug trafficking to the threat of systemic bias that influences our policies, the DEA is, in some ways, fighting the same battle fought by agents at the turn of the twentieth century as they began working to curtail the use of heroin and cocaine in medicines. While the ways in which we do so have changed, this is a fight that has been going on for generations—with the DEA at the forefront of that fight for decades.

CHAPTER NOTES

Chapter 4. Controversies of the DEA

1. Nick Wing, "12 of the Sketchiest Things the DEA Has Done While Waging the War on Drugs," HuffingtonPost.com, https://www.huffingtonpost.com/2014/10/23/dea-controversies_n_5992324.html.
2. Christopher Ingraham, "White people are more likely to deal drugs, but black people are more likely to get arrested for it," *Washington Post*, https://www.washingtonpost.com/news/wonk/wp/2014/09/30/white-people-are-more-likely-to-deal-drugs-but-black-people-are-more-likely-to-get-arrested-for-it/?noredirect=on&utm_term=.c961685lb9ae.
3. Zachary Siegel, "Why Does the DEA Continue to Fail Latin America?," The Fix, https://www.thefix.com/why-does-dea-continue-fail-latin-america.
4. Staff, "DEA's Colombia post jarred by misconduct probes," Associated Press, https://www.apnews.com/2f1efb591fb54d519c706792f0629763.
5. Mattathias Schwartz, "A Mission Gone Wrong," *New Yorker*, https://www.newyorker.com/magazine/2014/01/06/a-mission-gone-wrong.

Chapter 5. The Future of the DEA

1. Staff, "DEA announces "'360 Strategy' in Knoxville to address heroin, prescription drugs and violent crime," DEA.gov, https://www.dea.gov/press-releases/2018/09/25/dea-announces-360-strategy-knoxville-address-heroin-prescription-drugs.

GLOSSARY

Bureau of Internal Revenue The forerunner to the IRS, which was responsible for enforcing Prohibition.

cartels Organized networks through which drugs are taken around the world to be sold.

Controlled Substances Act A comprehensive set of laws passed in 1971 that addressed growing drug abuse in the United State and created the first drug scheduling system.

drug control The name given to a wide array of policies and initiatives designed to address drug abuse through prevention, law enforcement, and rehabilitation.

Drug Enforcement Administration Founded in 1973, the only federal agency devoted solely to drug control.

espionage The act of spying.

Food and Drug Administration Federal agency responsible for pharmaceuticals, among other substances, that works with the DEA on scheduling drugs.

Harrison Narcotics Tax Act Imposed taxes and regulations on some opium and cocaine products.

illicit substances Illegal drugs that can be abused.

narcotics Drugs that are or can be abused, but are not sold for medical reasons.

Pure Food and Drug Act The first drug regulation in the US, targeting cocaine and heroin by requiring labeling on products made with these substances.

GLOSSARY

Schedule I The most addictive and restricted of the tiers outlined under the CSA, with Schedule V as the most relaxed.

scheduling substances The process by which drugs and other substances are categorized according to the US system, which includes five ranks.

synthetic Describing substances not derived from nature, but made of chemical compounds.

zero-tolerance policy A form of drug control that does not take into account any information besides the criminal itself, providing little gray area when deciding sentencing and other punishments.

FURTHER READING

Books

Bagley, Bruce M., and Jonathan D. Rosen. *Drug Trafficking, Organized Crime, and Violence in the Americas Today.* Gainesville, FL: University of Florida Press, 2015.

Horning, Nicole. *Drug Trafficking: A Global Criminal Trade.* New York, NY: Lucent Books, 2018.

Rapine, Dawn. *A Career as a DEA Agent.* New York, NY: Rosen Publishing, 2016.

Websites

Drug Enforcement Administration

www.dea.gov

The DEA's official website includes the history of the organization, facts and figures about the drug trade in the United States, and information about careers with the DEA.

Office of National Drug Control Policy

www.whitehouse.gov/ondcp

The official website of the White House features press releases and official statements from the president on the issue of drug control in the United States.

United Nations Office on Drugs and Crime

www.unodc.org

The website of the UN's organization focused on fighting drugs and crime, the UNODC, features reports about drug trafficking as well as drug treatment, and offers statistics on the issue from not only the US, but countries around the world.

INDEX

A

accountability, lack of, 31, 35, 37, 41

Anti-Drug Abuse Act, 13

B

Bureau of Drug Abuse Control, 9

Bureau of International Narcotics Matters, 15

Bureau of Narcotics, 9

Bureau of Narcotics and Dangerous Drugs (BNDD), 9

Bureau of Prohibition, 9

C

Camarena, Enrique, 12

CIA, 38

cocaine, 7, 8, 12, 15, 24, 27, 28, 29, 30, 35, 42

Controlled Substances Act (CSA), 4, 9–10, 23

D

Department of Homeland Security (DHS), 6, 23

Department of Justice, 9

Department of the Treasury, 9

Drug Enforcement Administration (DEA)

    controversies, 6, 31–37
    duties of, 17–23
    future of, 38–42
    history of, 7–16
    overseas, 6, 10, 24–30
    overview of, 4–6

drug scheduling, 4, 9–10, 33, 38

E

ecstasy, 29

Escobar, Pablo, 29

Evans, D. Christopher, 41

F

FBI, 6, 20, 38

Food and Drug Administration (FDA), 4, 9

forensic financial analysis, 19–20

forfeiture operations, 23

H

Harrison Narcotics Tax Act, 8–9

heroin, 7–8, 10, 27, 28, 41, 42

I

ICE, 23

Interpol, 23

K

Kingpin Strategy, 15–16

M

mandatory minimum sentencing, 12

marijuana, 9, 16, 27, 33

Medellin cartel, 29

methamphetamine, 27

Morales, Evo, 35

N

Nixon, Richard, 4, 10, 12

Nongovernmental Organizations (NGOs), 29, 35

NSA, 41

O

Obama, Barack, 12

Operation Snowcap, 15

opioids, 16, 39, 41

opium, 8, 9, 15, 16, 27, 28–29, 41

organized crime, 6, 21, 30

P

privacy rights, 41

Prohibition, 9, 15

psychotropic drugs, 10

Pure Food and Drug Act, 7

R

racial disparities, 12, 33–34

Red Ribbon Campaign, 11–13

S

Search Bloc, 29

State Department, 15

sting operations, 6, 15, 23

T

360 Strategy, 39, 41

W

"war on drugs," 12